The Shift:
a spiritual guide for transforming your life and manifesting your dreams

by: Candace Victoria Mitchell

Copyright © 2017 CVM Enterprises

All rights reserved.

ABOUT THE AUTHOR

Candace V. Mitchell is an entrepreneur, author, and inspirational speaker. She currently serves as cofounder and CEO of Techturized Inc., a high tech hair care company based in Atlanta, GA. Their consumer brand, Myavana, is a personalized hair care service that recommends products, ingredients, and regimens based on scientific analysis of consumer's hair. She is a Forbes 30 Under 30 honoree in the Retail and E-Commerce category, Sephora Accelerate Fellow, named on WWD's Top 50 Beauty Innovators Under 40, and BET's Next In Class STEM Award Winner. She graduated from Georgia Tech in 2011 with a B.S. in Computer Science. Her company has been featured nationally on CNN, Headline News, BuzzFeed, The REAL daytime talk show, Marie Claire Magazine, MSNBC's Melissa Harris Perry show, ESSENCE magazine, Ebony Magazine, Black Enterprise, and Business Insider and many others. The visionary entrepreneur continues to help other minority and female entrepreneurs succeed as Entrepreneur-In-Residence for the Ascend 2020 Atlanta program.

Read more at candacevictoria.com. Follow on social media @thecvmlife.

THE SHIFT

Copyright © **2017 Candace V. Mitchell**

All rights reserved.

Published by **CVM Enterprises 2017**

Atlanta, Georgia

No parts of this publication may be reproduced, stored in a retrieval system, or transmitted in any form or by any means, electronic, mechanical, photocopying, recording, or otherwise, without the prior written permission of the copyright owner.

This book is sold subject to the condition that it shall not, by way of trade or otherwise, be lent, resold, hired out, or otherwise circulated without the publisher's prior consent in any form of binding or cover other than that in which it is published and without a similar condition including this condition being imposed on the subsequent purchaser. Under no circumstances may any part of this book be photocopied for resale.

Cover Photography: Monarch Butterfly by Sid Mosdell under a Creative Commons Attribution 4.0 International license (CC BY 4.0)

The thief comes only to steal and kill and destroy; I have come that they may have life, and have it more abundantly.

John 10:10

ACKNOWLEDGMENTS

To my readers:

My hope is for you to overcome the challenges of life and see your dreams come true, as I've been so blessed to see mine in plain sight. My prayer is that you be lifted up in every area needed so that you may experience a more abundant life.

Love,
Candace

What is THE SHIFT?

It's transforming your life…..
> from fear to faith
> from broken to healed
> from procrastination to action
> from self-doubt to self-belief
> from fear to love
> from depression to fullness
> from anxiety to peace
> from sorrow to joy
> from blame to responsibility
> from weakness to strength
> from trials to triumph
> from frustration to patience
> from sadness to happiness
> from employee to entrepreneur
> from lack to abundance
> from darkness to light.

Table of Contents

Intro — 10
    A Time For Everything — 10

Personal Shift — 23
    Self assessment — 24
    Introspective inventory — 26
    Affirmation & belief — 29

Professional Shift — 37
    Career change — 38
    Real leadership — 43
    Work ethic — 46

Mental Shift — 49
    Let go of the slavery mindset — 50
    Heal from your childhood wounds — 57
    Understand the real price of success — 60

Emotional Shift — 68
    Facing depression & anxiety — 69
    Breaking unhealthy attachments — 73
    Take responsibility for your life — 76

Financial Shift — 80
    The value of money — 81
    Your relationship with money — 83
    Income generation — 84

Relational Shift	**88**
Circle of support	89
Association	91
Disassociation	93
Spiritual Shift	**97**
Overcoming fear	98
Finding faith	99
Seeing purpose in your pain	102
Outro	**104**
So let's begin the shift	104
The Shift Plan	107
Personal Shift	107
Professional Shift	108
Mental Shift	108
Emotional Shift	109
Financial Shift	110
Relational Shift	110
Spiritual Shift	111

Intro

A Time For Everything

It's now been 5 ½ years since I've stepped out on faith as an entrepreneur to begin growing the business of my dreams. A once 24 year old driving across the country from Dallas to Atlanta to move back home with a car packed to the max with as many of my possessions that I could take. My next stop was to crash on a mattress in my mom's living room and prepare to begin my first day as a full-time entrepreneur walking through the doors of the Flashpoint startup accelerator based at The Georgia Institute of Technology. Looking back on those times, I now have a deeper awareness of who I am, how I've been able to endure this journey, and how I have been awakened to a new level of existence that is pivotal in bringing the unseen to the visible plane of life. The original version of this book was a collection of reflections and revelations that came to me during the month of December 2015 when I decided to take a month off from my company after suffering from depression and anxiety which stemmed from an emotional rollercoaster of the highs and lows of entrepreneurship, dealing with the fluctuation of mountaintop successes and debilitating disappointments, and ultimately driving myself to exhaustion and emptiness. It was a moment of surrender where God was telling me to rest and I could do nothing but be obedient. Little did I know that it would be the month before the most pivotal moments of my entrepreneurial career.

This inward reflection and time of surrender is what manifested a grander reality. The month following this time of reflection, January 2016, my company was on national TV being featured on The Real, I was named to the 2016 Forbes 30 Under 30 List, I won BET's Next In Class Award for the STEM category that would be featured on BET Honors, and we were contacted by Sephora to apply to their inaugural entrepreneurship program, Sephora Accelerate, in which we were later chosen as 1 of 8 companies from the United States, Canada, and Latin America who represented the future of beauty to join this special program to aid the growth of female led beauty businesses. Surrendering to God has led to a shift of manifesting greater blessings. The new edition of this book is infused with more knowledge and revelations from the last 2 years of my journey, but from a more awakened level of interpretation from what I call "a better version of myself" because of my growth and mindfulness of what it takes to be a successful entrepreneur. The key to getting through life well is evolution and recognizing how you're evolving then making changes accordingly.

The weight of what led to the more traumatic stages of my journey was due to an accumulation of stress, being a people pleaser, neglecting self-care, managing other people's expectations, and continuous sacrifices that chipped away at my overall well-being. I have battled things I never imagined I would, but it's transformed me in many ways as a woman and as an entrepreneur. I have experienced moments of pure joy from successes and breakthroughs against all odds. I have also experienced very low moments where I felt like my back was against the wall and I had no one to turn to. In those dark nights of the soul, I always reminded myself that weeping may endure for a night but joy comes in the morning. Times when we're experiencing our greatest challenges are typically right before our greatest breakthroughs. Times when we're ready to pack up and give up are moments when we're three feet from gold. I'm thankful that I came to know Jesus Christ as my Lord and Savior when I was in high school which is when it occurred to me that He died for me to overcome anything that I could possibly face in life. I am totally sure that it was nothing my God and my mother's prayers that allowed me to persevere and graduate from Georgia Tech which before being an entrepreneur was the hardest thing I had ever accomplished. Because of the presence of God and my salvation through Jesus Christ, I can always be assured that whatever I am forced to deal with or overcome, that it is already done and has already been defeated.

I had to overcome the shame of struggling silently, which many of us do. It's more than just having a superwoman or superman complex. My experience is that sometimes you just don't know how to express it or who to express it to if you don't already go to a licensed therapist. You keep going and going and going like the energizer bunny and for seemingly good reasons. We all feel very strongly about the vision and purpose that we're called to, but most of the time we try to do too many things in our own power. We forget to practice self-care along the way. I came to a point where God just had to help me unpack all of the emotions and issues that I never dealt with because of the daily grind and all of the responsibilities that

I felt were always so much more important than myself. God then asked me, "how can you endure this journey I will take you on with these burdens you're carrying? It's time for a shift to be all that I am calling you to be." So this time of surrender led to beautiful moments of self-reflection in every area of my life so that I could fully receive what God had planned for me.

There's a beautiful quote by Oprah Winfrey that says, "Create the highest, grandest vision possible for your life, because you become what you believe." I always knew that I was great, even the days and moments when I didn't quite get things right. I quickly discovered that the capacity to tap into our highest, grandest self - the greatness that we so constantly seek - is all in our mindset and what we truly believe about ourselves. We have already been blessed with the things we need to build a great life. It all has its appointed time of manifestation in the world that coincides with your own personal awakening. As I reflected on my journey of entrepreneurship, I realized very quickly that there were several things that I had to intentionally shift in order to endure what was ahead of me. I was experiencing full circle moments to re-learn these lessons as I was entering my cocoon and a full metamorphosis of the mind. This shift changed my spirit and touched my soul. I knew that fully facing these things about myself was the only true way to achieve the success that I know is in my destiny. There are so many instances in which we get in our own way because we are held back by our own fears that we're never fully ready to confront or acknowledge. I realized that to achieve what I believed - the highest, grandest vision possible for my life - this shift was necessary and waiting on me to trust God to fulfill.

A shift can happen voluntarily or involuntarily. Some we can intentionally, prayerfully prepare for. Some catch us by surprise like a miraculous accomplishment or an unfortunate tragedy. Both are delicately designed by God. It's up to us to decide how to deal with or be dealt with. We all have the power to choose how we invite the shift into our lives.

I am a woman who had a vision and made the decision to move forward in faith which opened a path beyond my wildest dreams. I endeavor to use my spiritual gifts of faith, wisdom, and encouragement to help others along this path. As I learn, I desire to teach. I am a firm believer that as you awaken to your purpose and greet challenges with perseverance, you will experience personal transformation. As you identify the specific gifts, skills, talents, and resources that allow you to live out your purpose and give those to others, the communities in which you dwell will also experience transformation and you will receive divine compensation from the universe. So it is a certain fact that the world is also waiting on you to be all that you've been called to be.

The next level you wish to attain, however you define it – financially, professionally, emotionally, spiritually, personally – is waiting for you to awaken to your purpose, take action on what's revealed to you, and continuously share your gifts and experiences with others. When you're operating in your purpose, you naturally and authentically bless others in a way that creates value in their life and adds value to yours. It's for their well-being that they can be blessed by what you have - what God created in you from birth. It's the gift that keeps on giving. I endeavor to continually share my gifts with others to create new value in this world that leaves it better in which I inherited.

I knew that it was going to take a new thought process to get to a new level. A shift in every sense of the word. Once you do this, you'll realize that you had the power this whole time. Once you awaken to it and believe in it, nothing in your life will be the same. You will be unstoppable. I welcome you to an experience of reflection and application as you make the shift to transform your life and manifest your dreams.

There is a time for everything. God tells us this in Ecclesiastes 3:1-8:

> There is a time for everything,
> and a season for every activity under the heavens:
> a time to be born and a time to die,
> a time to plant and a time to uproot,
> a time to kill and a time to heal,
> a time to tear down and a time to build,
> a time to weep and a time to laugh,
> a time to mourn and a time to dance,
> a time to scatter stones and a time to gather them,
> a time to embrace and a time to refrain from embracing,
> a time to search and a time to give up,

a time to keep and a time to throw away,
a time to tear and a time to mend,
a time to be silent and a time to speak,
a time to love and a time to hate,
a time for war and a time for peace.

We must understand that there is a sowing time and a harvest time. A time in which God is preparing us and a time in which God calls us to take what we've learned and put it into action, oftentimes by faith. The ability for us to discern when these times come is directly correlated to our willingness to be still, listen for God's voice, and follow His call. So many of us miss our divine assignments and instructions because we are too busy to make time for God or always drown out His voice with the hustle and bustle of life. Our times of appointment are often missed because we also hold ourselves back with things like bad habits, fear, disobedience, and pride. Yet all things still work together for our good and God will create a path to account for these shortcomings. You will continue to experience the same cycles until you break them by submitting to God's plans. And His plans for you are good, more than you've ever dreamed of. Your ability to achieve is directly correlated to your ability to receive. We cannot receive what God is waiting to bless us with until we replace fear with faith, disobedience with the will to obey, and pride with readiness to humble ourselves. My wish is for everyone to gain the courage to follow your dreams at all costs and surrender to the moments in which God brings things to your attention in order to make a change. It's a daily art in overcoming fear and persevering through challenges, yet it's everything it takes to make a shift that makes the rest of your life the best of your life.

Many things hold us back from taking that first step on the path to our dreams, yet I declare this read to be an awakening to all who lay eyes on these words that there is greater waiting on you to make this shift in your life. A lot of it is personal, things like self-esteem, belief in yourself, knowing that you're good enough, overcoming mental blocks, wounds from your childhood, failures, you name it. We all have a laundry list of memories and hurts that have kept us in bondage and "disqualify" us from truly believing that we can experience the success we envision. I wrestled with these things on a daily basis, but came to a point where I told myself I would no longer let negativity plague my mind. We all have experiences that leave us bruised and feeling unqualified, but you can also decide not to operate from that frame of mind. I will not let "them" stop me from doing what I know God has placed on my heart to do. Through the power of intention, we can all make our visions plain and move forward in truly making it a reality.

There comes a time in life when you evolve from just using your skills and talents to operating in your anointing. You transform from a doer to a seeker and from striving to being. God didn't give you a dream to intimidate you with the impossible, He gave you a dream to show you all things are possible. Once you tap into that, you'll realize you have all that you need to make a shift to seeing your dreams become a reality. You won't have to run on your own strength. The universe will conspire to bring your dreams to life on Earth. The dream that you so earnestly seek is actually a glimpse of your destiny waiting to be revealed in plain sight. Since the beginning of time, God has always wanted all of His children to live life more abundantly. That's why he planned the coming of His son, Jesus Christ, to pay the price for our sins and all the ways we screw things up on a daily basis just so that we can still experience His grace. He demonstrated that He won't let us get in our own way, that we can always be saved by grace at any moment to fully live out who He's called us to be. We are His children, we are His heirs. When you refuse to worry, but choose to surrender and rest in the finished work of Christ, you will see the manifestation of your blessing.

So let's begin the shift to a higher level of living.

Personal Shift

Do you know who you really are?

Self assessment

I made a personal commitment to better myself - the shift from avoiding my flaws to embracing them for true change.

As you awaken on the inside, what you seek will manifest on the outside. It's important to remember that everything first starts from within. I took an honest account of how I felt in every area of my life and gave myself a grade from A-F. We must recognize that how we perform in life stems from how we feel about ourselves. That is the foundation. Since I'm being honest and transparent, here's how I scored:

> Spiritually - B
> Mentally - C
> Emotionally - C
> Physically - F
> Financially - C

Take a pulse on these areas in your life and rate yourself. Then, take time to think about why you've rated yourself in the manner in which you did. Consider ways that you can take action for improvement and determine what's the first step you can take starting today to be your best self. It can be things like having consistent morning devotional and prayer time, making space in your schedule for a romantic companion, getting in the gym more often, changing your diet, taking vitamins, creating a budget, etc. My improvements began mentally as I discovered the ways that I was limiting myself with defeating thoughts and how I consistently put myself last which damaged my health and well-being. I was also overworking and doing everything myself. That led to poor delegation, exhaustion, and disappointment. Once you determine the root of your actions, you'll see how it affects every area of your life. But the good thing is addressing the root leads to instant improvement in every area of your life. Don't be afraid to face the hard stuff. We may be bruised, but not broken. We can always be better and do better. Since then, I've changed my life dramatically and here's now how I rate myself:

> Spiritually - A
> Mentally - A
> Emotionally - A
> Physically - B
> Financially - B

Introspective inventory

I took an introspective inventory of my strengths and weaknesses - the shift from passive awareness to intentional application.

Taking inventory of your strengths and weaknesses oftentimes provides a clear picture of how you best operate, what you need to improve on, and who you need in your life to complement you. Knowing yourself first should be the determining factor in how you choose a partner and who you need on your team to go into business. This also includes knowing your values, your expectations for commitment, and having a sound judgment of character. It's a necessity to know what your strengths and weaknesses are so that you know what role is truly best for you and how to compensate for the things that you're not the best at. It's very rare to have the capacity to build and implement your ideas on your own completely. We must broaden our awareness of the true need to build a team of people to help execute. We must ensure that we're making smart choices that come down to the ability to do the job and possessing the right culture/character fit. We must be willing to share the spotlight and not want certain positions for our own shine. We must expand our capacity to trust others while implementing measurable goals. We have to be intentional in how we build relationships to build strong partnerships that stand the test of time. Just because someone has a bomb resume and presumably "the full package" doesn't mean they have the heart, character, and integrity to bring the vision to its true fullness. Always go back to your strengths, weaknesses, and values as a good sounding board for who will be great complements to build a strong team and create a fulfilling life. Egos must be left at the door and service should be the core goal. Always trust your intuition and your gut if someone gives off bad energy or shows you their true colors. As Maya Angelou once said, "when someone shows you who they are, believe them the first time."

I acknowledged the mistakes that I made in choosing the right people to work with as lessons learned in building my team in the future. I became more aware of my abilities, but also my limitations. It's just as important to know the limits of what you can handle and have the ability to communicate that, even it means navigating through conflict and changes. I didn't get this right away. I had to learn the hard way. I actually had to endure some painful experiences in order for God to really bring this to light for me. Oftentimes moving into a new level of your life will demand a different version of you. God does His job in refining you to be the person you need to be to fully receive the new level of blessing and to make better decisions in the future.

When God gives you a fresh start, don't duplicate past mistakes. Don't let time drift by so far that you allow yourself to fall into a slump, a pit, a dark place and wonder how you got there. Take introspective inventory along the way. I ask myself every week the following questions: Am I becoming the woman I've envisioned myself to be? Am I creating the life I want to have? Have I voiced all concerns that I'm experiencing? What lessons am I learning that I can start applying right away? I keep a constant pulse on my answers and heart demeanor towards the inquiry. I'm reminded of what Steve Jobs also asked himself in the mirror every day, 'If today were the last day of my life, would I want to do what I am about to do today?' And whenever the answer has been 'No', for too many days in a row, I know I need to change something." And The Shift is all about recognizing that you have the power to make that change.

Affirmation & belief

I created affirmations and renewed belief in myself - the shift from lingering defeating thoughts to active empowering thoughts.

Please believe that once I knew that a shift was preparing to take place, I've been on my knees praying every night and every morning. I prayed for a renewed sense of belief in myself and to triumph against every trial and attack that may come my way. To bring a dream to pass, you have to acknowledge that there are several realms of awareness and action that require our attention. We cannot conceive what our mind isn't willing to believe. You have to see yourself being that trailblazer, innovator, change agent, and success story. Once you see it, you have to truly believe it in order for it to manifest in reality. God has to see your faith in action. And once He sees it, you have to allow Him to stretch it. That may be the only true way for you to receive what you believe. It reminds me of a quote from my favorite author, Marianne

Williamson, "Who am I to be brilliant, gorgeous, talented and fabulous? Actually, who are you not to be? You are a child of God." I had to see myself as all of those things to activate my gifts and my worthiness.

Who am I to think my company will transform a billion dollar industry in a way that has never been done before? Who are you to think that you will impact millions of people in this world with your ideas, your talents, your gifts, and your creations? Actually, who are you not to be? We are children of the Most High God who created the entire universe! And we were created in His image. This should be our automatic response when we think about affirming ourselves and believing in ourselves. Now ask yourself, "do I really believe that I will achieve what I'm seeking to accomplish?" Observe your response to that question. Would you score 100% if graded on your belief in yourself?

If you fall short of that, it just shows you the room in which you need to grow. It's being pointed out to you so that God can show you how much He can move in your life to bring your dreams to fruition because He planted them within you in the first place. Also consider what may be holding you back from truly believing in yourself. Create a consistent stream of consciousness that empowers you throughout your day.

Sometimes fear steps in the way of our growth in faith. It's a natural thing, the world is plagued with fear. One thing that always brings me back and truly creates a fearless spirit within me is rooted in this scripture:

> But you will not leave in haste
> or go in flight;
> for the Lord will go before you,
> the God of Israel will guard you from behind.
> - Isaiah 52:12

How would you feel if you truly knew that God has already gone before you and the vision you have in your mind has already been done in the timeless nature of the universe and God is entrusting you to increase your belief in order for it to manifest here in the Earth. That's what it means when we say "it's already done!" Our present place of promise causes us to draw near to God for direction. It's perfectly designed through prayer to ask and understand, "what should I do to move forward? Is there something I should do differently?" That's when a "coincidental" message or person comes along our path and provides a breakthrough. He provides guidance for our personal growth and for the path we should take in our lives. I'm always affirmed and comforted by Psalm 23 when it says:

> The Lord is my shepherd, I lack nothing.
> He makes me lie down in green pastures,
> He leads me beside quiet waters,
> He refreshes my soul.
> He guides me along the right paths
> for his name's sake.
> Even though I walk
> through the darkest valley,
> I will fear no evil,
> for you are with me;
> your rod and your staff,
> they comfort me.
> You prepare a table before me
> in the presence of my enemies.
> You anoint my head with oil;
> my cup overflows.
> Surely your goodness and mercy will follow
> me all the days of my life,
> and I will dwell in the house of the Lord
> forever.

See - God has your back! He sent a Savior that has walked in our shoes and walks with us everyday of our lives. Even if you feel like your time has passed because it's taken you so long to truly believe in yourself for whatever reason you've been tainted, we always have a chance to begin again, more wisely. I make the conscious choice to be great everyday, no matter what I face. I understand the trials of life are allowed to help us learn, grow, evolve, and transform. It provides a chance to believe in yourself even more. Affirm yourself even more. Make a shift to allow the challenging times strengthen you and not crush you. Work those faith muscles! God's plans for us are good. Now there are times when you may feel stuck because the wins may be far and few in between and you spend most of your time tackling challenges. It's okay. Continue to pray through it for in due time, the humble will be exalted.

I remember sitting down and thinking about who God has called me to be. Some powerful words came to mind and I chose to embrace them and not be scared thinking, "really God? That's me?" Yep, it is. I am that I am. Businesswoman. Teacher. Inspirational Speaker. Computer Scientist. Humanitarian.

My personal testimony is that I've battled with self-esteem the majority of my life. I actually felt complete for the first time at the age of 28. I'm not afraid to admit that I've struggled with this. So many of us do. Let this be your wake up call that you are already whole and complete! I've been defeated by the spirit of comparison and lack for far too long. This has been from an internal longing and also external pressures at times. It's affected everything from my body image, my confidence in my abilities, and my presence as a minority and woman in the technology industry. Let's just make it known right now that you don't need anyone's validation to be who you're called to be. You're perfect just as you are.

I created this affirmation to defeat every negative lingering thought to replace with an empowering thought:

I am worthy of what I dream of. I am more than capable of accomplishing it.

A personal example is me overcoming my insecurities to develop a commanding presence when pitching on stage that attracted over $200,000 in cash and services for our startup company. Every time I stepped on stage I believed that I would win. I never knew I had the power to captivate an audience in this way until I was forced to actually dig inside and use it. It's purely a demonstration of confidence, clarity, and charisma. My earnest prayer every time was, "Lord, empower me to touch the hearts and minds of this audience and move in their spirits to feel the same passion that I feel inside." When you pitch you're delivering a message of a great vision and representing your company as the perfect team to bring it to life. You build trust and confidence in a matter of minutes or seconds. You help others envision a new, brighter, better world with what you've created and they believe in your abilities to execute in bringing it to fruition. And that's what wins pitch competitions. That is the power of belief.

Professional Shift

Are you really doing what you're truly called to do?

Career change

I prayerfully prepared for my career change - the shift from a full-time employee to a startup entrepreneur.

I remember sitting at my desk at my first corporate job after college and thinking to myself that I was so much bigger than this cubicle. I loved my role and the company that I worked for. I was excelling and developed great rapport with everyone that I worked with. I just felt like I was out of alignment with my greater calling. When these feelings occur, it's a sign to start digging deeper to see where they may lead. I started a spiritual journey of discovering my true purpose in life by reading the book, The Purpose Driven Life by Rick Warren. I then started to receive a series of signs from God that led me to my passion for entrepreneurship and the "hair idea" that I worked on in college. Those signs prepared me to take a leap of faith that I had no idea would transpire at that phase of my life. In a period of only three months, I found myself saying goodbye to that cubicle and opening a new chapter as an entrepreneur.

I would like to share my resignation letter from Corporate America when I knew the time had arrived to follow the path of building my own business:

Dear Managers, (names have been removed for privacy)

I've recently been awakened to a higher calling for my life. It is the point in which my natural talents, learned skills, and personal experiences have intersected with the potential to meet the needs of others. While this has appeared to me most unexpectedly and warrants an unconventional decision to make, it radiates with an illuminating beam to follow the path in which it has enlightened, a path in which I feel compelled by the Lord above to take....a demonstration of my obedience to His will for my life.

Oftentimes we make plans, and those plans are disrupted. It is natural to then adopt a perplexed mindset and grab the pieces to put them back together. However, the spiritual development that I have undergone recognizes this as God's providential way of getting my attention and providing an opportunity that comes once in a lifetime.

During my junior year of college, I entered a competition to invent an idea that meets a current need in the world. Harnessing my interests and experiences as an African- American woman as well as my intellectual prowess in computer science, I decided to blend two fields together -- hair care and technology. This product was a software analysis that can predict which products are best for your hair, based on your hair DNA. Fast forward two years later, during a recent visit back home, I was approached by a former professor who guided me during the competition and inquired about if I continued to work on the idea. He also connected me with others whom he knew had similar interests.

The result of the connections made and the impromptu encouragement to re-explore the concept has miraculously provided the opportunity to participate in a startup accelerator program at Georgia Tech. Flashpoint offers entrepreneurial education and access to experienced mentors, experts, and investors in an exciting, immersive, shared-learning workspace to develop your product and pitch it for funding. It is also most likely that there will be few other African-Americans, especially African-American women, participating in the program. The opportunity to defy the odds of the double minority and revolutionize the hair care industry through the power of technology is one worth taking a risk for. We are required to participate in the program this summer, beginning on June 4th, which lasts for 3 months.

I believe that this is a divine intervention for me to follow my passion and impact the lives of others in a greater way. I'm so connected to the concept of harnessing the hair care industry and the strong role that hair plays in a woman's identity to promote empowerment. I yearn to reach women in their day-to-day lives and inspire them to live their best life and always know that they are fearless and beautiful.

This is a very bittersweet decision because I love PepsiCo dearly. The experience has been nothing but wonderful. I truly looked forward to all the things to come as I continued to grow in my role and work with the various teams in my different rotations. I also felt connected to the performance with purpose mission and was always truly proud to work with a company with such values.

With everything to consider, I believe that this step is a small piece in God's bigger plan. It is a difficult decision to make, and I would surely appreciate all the support possible in allowing me to fulfill this dream. I will share my experience with PepsiCo whenever and wherever I have the chance as an essential chapter in my life's journey, an amazing company to work for, and a brand to be cherished. With every aspect of my being, I sincerely thank you.

With my deepest gratitude,
Candace

It goes without saying that my preparation for a career change was a spiritual journey. I find it hard to consider any other way to be prepared to step out into the unknown. I had never started a company before. I had no idea if we would succeed or fail. I just knew that I had to be obedient in taking that first step, making a shift professionally from Corporate America to entrepreneurship. Establishing a great spiritual foundation will sustain you in any change you make in your life. I challenge you to reflect on your purpose as your guiding light to your next move. It will definitely ensure that it's your best move.

Real leadership

I committed to work on my leadership skills - shifting from company associate to CEO.

A book that I purchased shortly after high school graduation was titled Jesus, CEO. It was a beautiful compilation of examples in which Jesus exhibited servant leadership amongst His people and provided a great model in which to follow as the leader of a company. I thought I would glide right through what I had learned and put it directly into practice. Boy was I wrong. My leadership ability was met with stubborn resistance from those around me. It was a storm from day one. A delicate time of growing into my purpose as a leader was tainted and attacked with egotistical intentions. So many things prevented me from truly being the leader I know I am called to be. And at the same time, I knew they were experiences I had to go through - to groom me, shape me, mold me, and push me to cling to God more. We may not have it all together on day one, but every day and every experience presents a new way to develop into who you are called to be. The moral of the story is that I'm still standing. My strength is that I know that I'm not perfect, I am just willing to be used by God and willing to work on myself to progress and grow. He doesn't call the qualified, He qualifies the called. He creates experiences that helps you learn what skills you need to cultivate. He presented challenges that created a clear list of skills to develop and improve on. I could have decided to throw in the towel and say I'm not cut out for this. But I believed in my heart that the story didn't stop there and there was more to me.

Do you ever believe there is more to you? Do you sit and think I'm way bigger than my current circumstances? Or declare I know this is not it for me? When those thoughts come, it's preparing a way for you to identify the gap in who you are today and who you need to be tomorrow. Don't be afraid to cultivate those skills, even when you make mistakes. God loves you too much to allow you to stay the same. Failure presents the opportunity to begin again more wisely and it's a stepping stone for future success.

I remember several times when I would look around the room with the realization that I was the only woman or only minority. I thought surely times have changed in leadership with more gender and racial diversity but I've been consistently surprised and reminded of the dual nature of my journey in building a successful company but also breaking barriers for women and minorities in leadership in the technology and business arenas. I've learned that a true leader is willing to be used for the greater good of humanity. As women, we are coming for our rightful positions in leadership. As minorities, we are no longer succumbing to the systemic barriers of knowledge and monetary resources in bringing more wealth to our communities. It brings a new motivation for success when you know that you're opening doors for others to come through and blazing a trail that leads to greater opportunities for those that come after you. It brings a whole new attitude to exhibit perseverance with purpose that will impact your entire generation and the generation after you. It brings a whole new meaning to real leadership and makes enduring failures so much more gratifying because of the lessons learned that you can apply and share to make a difference for others.

Work ethic

I leveled up on my work ethic without complaints or excuses - the shift from clocking out to doing whatever it takes to get the job done.

We must understand that there comes a time when we have to be willing to do whatever it takes, period. This will be a time of stretching yourself and ignoring barriers as only illusions. You must refuse to take no for an answer. God is building your muscles. It will also challenge you to think. Do you really want increase? Do you really want the limits off? Do you really want to enlarge your territory? We get caught up in the prosperity gospel and sometimes we want the rewards without the work. Remember, faith without works is dead. Take a moment to ask yourself have you truly put in the work to receive what you believe. And let's not put the term work in a box of just reference to labor. God wants to see you put in work by spending time with Him, studying His word so that you can pass the tests and graduate into your breakthrough. Have the wisdom to understand when it comes to work that there is a time for sowing and a time for reaping.

An affirmation that is dear to my heart is: I go confidently in the direction of my dreams and live the life that I've imagined.
- Henry David Thoreau

What does it mean to go confidently? It means in a manner filled with tenacity, heart, and relentless action to see what you believe. A person who moves confidently is rarely complaining and uses every lesson as a bridge to the next victory. Let your work ethic demonstrate your confidence that in due time you will reap your harvest if you do not give up. Plant those seeds of discipline, follow through, and dedication. The harvest will be plentiful if you patiently wait for it.

Mental Shift

"Why do you stay in prison when the door is so wide open?
- Rumi

Let go of the slavery mindset

I recognized old cycles of slavery mentality and uprooted the habits that held me back from my breakthrough - the shift from suffering to breaking free.

I am an avid journaler and have been chronicling my life experiences since I was in college. Because I've kept this up well into my entrepreneurship years, I am able to look back on certain time periods and observe my mindset. There was a specific financial goal that I was seeking to meet at the time and I became extremely perplexed by the fact that I would fall short every single time. I could not figure it out for the life of me and ended up having a complete breakdown. What occurred to me after studying the things I wrote about over the past year were these cyclical feelings of guilt and shame from previous mistakes and resorting to taking on more debt. I came to the stark realization that my mentality was the main thing keeping me from meeting my goals. How could I excel in meeting my financial goals with the low vibrational thoughts of guilt and shame? The energy that I was subconsciously emitting was pulling me down and keeping me in a stagnant place. Your mentality is the greatest indicator of whether or not you will see your dreams come to fruition. As a society and culture, we have been conditioned to be numb to our inner world. We've been taught to be externally driven. It's all about achievement and how things look on the outside. Why do we avoid looking inside? It keeps us in a state of bondage and not truly experiencing freedom.

Jay-Z recently dropped the following thought provoking lyrics that kept it real in a way that shows how he's been able to ascend to be the icon that he is today. In the song "I Got The Keys" he states, "Until you own your own you can't be free. Until you own your own you can't be me. How we still slaves in 2016?" He brings up an urgent point that "the culture" is still operating like slaves. We do the same things every weekend like drink, smoke, and party. We hustle, hustle, hustle, and never learn that life is a flow and is always pulling us back to how we're anointed to thrive where we naturally excel in life, but we ignore it just to stay on the grind. We flaunt and floss the latest fashions and make it a top expenditure on our "I Made It" wish list. We go to events for the sake of going and being seen. When will we learn to invest in ourselves? When will we learn to own our own assets and make that a top priority instead of continuously making other people rich? When was the last time you truly invested in your gifts and talents? If you made a list of your assets, what do you really own?

Half of the battle is that we're not taught these things growing up. I can tell that in the families of some of my peers who are of European and Asian descent that they have handed down assets and wealth from generation to generation which places them in a position of wealth creating mindset without the worries of paying off debt, getting through school, and gaining access to capital to start their businesses. Although we are starting at a disadvantage, I do believe that we are the generation that can start changing things. This change first starts in the way that you think. Mark today as the day you start changing the decisions that you make to only be in alignment with contributing to your future freedom and the freedom for our families.

We've been oppressed, but now it's our time to rise. We've been overlooked, but we won't be ignored.

We've been misunderstood, but now it's time for the world to recognize, we are indeed geniuses and the tides are turning for more of us to bridge the divide and contribute our greatness to the world. There is genius level talent within all of us. In the Black community, we've had our own unique plight in creating wealth but it has nothing to do with the quality of our gifts, talents, and abilities. It's gaining access to the resources, tools, mentors, and advisors that can help shepherd those of us who are ready for real change. But first we must change our minds in order to reach the promised land.

In the books of Exodus and Numbers we read about how God set the Israelites free from slavery in Egypt. Led by Moses, they miraculously crossed the Red Sea, but then the greatest remembrance of this story is that the Israelites wandered in the wilderness for 40 years. Many people do not realize that it was designed to be only an 11 day journey. The plight of the Israelites and what held them back was due to their disobedience and unbelief in God. They complained the entire time and practically gave Moses hell as a leader. Sadly, God did not allow that generation to see the Promised Land. They all died in the wilderness. Like many people, they walked by sight and not by faith, and their unbelief displeased God. There were only 2 people that did inherit the Promised Land and they were the only 2 leaders from the 12 tribes who were sent out into the land as spies and came back with faith in believing that they could possess the land. These 2 faithful spies, Joshua and Caleb, survived and inherited God's promise because they believed and let go of their slavery mentality.

There are other ways the slave mentality may be present, such as: waiting on permission from others, entitlement, carrying the heavy weight of burdens and doing things in your own strength, talking about others instead of focusing on your own goals, waiting on someone else to change your life, thinking that the only way to earn money is through a 9 to 5 job (instead of through serving others in a way that can be monetized), amongst others. Operating from a mindset of freedom means that you take the initiative personally to accomplish the desires of your heart, you assume responsibility for your life, you ask for help knowing that you will be fully supported in some form or fashion, you offer help to others, and seek the path to solving a pain or need in the market of your interest. A free mind is led to seek all avenues to see their dream come true whether it be through writing, coding, starting a business, creating dope experiences and events for others, innovating the marketplace, inventing new products, authoring new books, starting a new club or organization -- whatever your heart desires. It doesn't matter if you succeed or fail, the main difference is that you try. Trying is what separates the good from the great. We were all created as "good" in the image of God, but only the great ones ascend in cultivating their God-given gifts, talents, interests, and desires into the world in service to others. Greatness is the embodiment of a mind that believes, attempts, revises, speaks their truth, tries again and again, takes risks, owns responsibilities and works hard -- all things that the average person has been conditioned to avoid.

Here's a prayer for you if you struggle with having any aspect of the slavery mentality and unbelief that God can do the amazing things that you're dreaming of:

> **God, please help me with my unbelief. Please unblock anything that is hindering my sight to see you do the impossible in my life. Please renew my mind from any part of my mentality that keeps me in bondage. Please restore the vision that**

you have placed on my life and give me not only the ability to see it but to believe in it. Amen.

I have been blessed to be led by my Pastor, Dr. Bryan E. Crute from Destiny Metropolitan Worship Church throughout my entrepreneurial journey. I knew I wanted to be an entrepreneur since college and several of his sermons have guided me every step of the way. In one of his recent sermons titled, "Get Ready For The Upgrade" he shared some of his learnings from being inspired by Bishop T.D. Jakes recent book called Soar about how there are so many people who are praying and believing in God but may not see the manifestation of their prayers. What he discovered is that oftentimes we are praying for the wrong things like to pay this bill or get this opportunity when we should be praying bigger like expanding your income or becoming a creator of jobs through your entrepreneurial ideas. He shared an amazing analogy about praying for tables and chairs instead of praying for trees. When you see the trees that have been planted, you will see the tables and chairs. We must change our perspectives and ask for deeper insight. Stop looking at your problem and see the solution to your problem. It's the shift from consumers in our mentality to producers in our mentality. Pastor Crute passionately shared how God has given us the abilities to reap what we are seeking. We are already wealthy. We are rich with gifts, talents, and experiences. God is leading us to look inside ourselves instead of begging because we have been blind to how God is really providing for us. We have the gifts to produce so we don't have to beg and complain about what we don't have but start thanking Him for what we do have.

God has placed in the Earth everything that you and I need to fulfill our callings. Be resourceful or get around someone who is resourceful so that you can learn how to be. Let today be the last day of a poverty mentality.

Heal from your childhood wounds

I dealt with pains I experienced as a child that were influencing my behavior in adulthood - the shift from being controlled by the past to healing my present and future.

The root of the wrong mindset is typically found in our childhood wounds. This is a very sensitive topic because it can immediately invoke the need for blame for why we are the way that we are. But that's not the purpose. I'm bringing up this topic to raise awareness around the realization that the majority of people are carrying around hurts and wounds from things that happened in their childhood and *may not be conscious of the fact that it's affecting their behavior even as an adult today*. This is true for even people in their 50s, 60s, and 70s - unfortunately most take these pains to the grave. Different things may still be affecting us such as abandonment, anger, loss, perfectionism, competition, being left out, violence in the home, rejection, shame, humiliation, betrayal, and others. Many of us have an inner child that is still yearning to be healed. It's important to address this as soon as you realize that it may be happening to you in order to start operating from the right frame of mind.

I first realized that I still carried the struggles of childhood wounds when I was having a hard time communicating my needs to other people. I noticed my repetitive response to inquiries or offers for help which would always be, *"I'm fine."* I'm sure many of you could relate. It wasn't until one day I sat in a state of helplessness and said to myself, "I'm not fine." And then I asked myself, "Why?". What was revealed to me was that I still have not healed from certain things that I felt had plagued my life as a little girl which was insecurity, unworthiness, shame, and self-doubt. As a protective mechanism, I impeded my ability to be vulnerable and ask for help. I experienced these things in my life for various reasons and I "thought" I had somewhat tackled these things because I first saw the adverse affects of this when it came to my relationships with men and different dating experiences. But then I realized that these things will rear its ugly head in every area of our lives until they are rightfully uprooted. When I realized how it was affecting how I operate in my business I promptly took a step back and sought out a spiritual mentor. These were strongholds that I knew I needed the presence of an outside perspective to really help me grow out of. I believe in the power of intercessory prayer and asking God to uproot these feelings that were intended for evil and have a negative effect on how I think. I immediately realized that my blocks in communication and asking for what I really want was because deep down inside there was a wound of feeling unworthy, a wound of being insecure, a wound of being ashamed, a wound of doubting myself. I purposefully started to set out time daily and weekly to heal my heart and my mind from the things that affected my mentality and I've been free every since. It's a glorious feeling that I desire to see everyone feel for themselves.

Understand the real price of success

I created my own definition of success - the shift from what society defines as successful to understanding what success really is.

Success has been simplified into a series of steps with a magical outcome without the context of time, effort, and personal definition. It causes us to be measured to other people's standard of success without knowing what would really make us happy. You must define what success means for yourself and stay focused on achieving the goal you set before you. You have to stay committed and be in it for the long haul. To whom much is given, much is required. There is a price to pay in order to succeed. From someone who has been "in the trenches" for some time now, I reflected on five different things that uncover the real PRICE of success:

P - Perseverance

Albert Einstein said, "It's not that I'm so smart, it's just that I stay with problems longer." Perseverance gives you the ability to endure obstacles with a relentless attitude to never give up. There are countless examples of industry-defining, world-renowned, amazing individuals who've created brands, businesses, and experiences that we love that exude the spirit of perseverance. If Howard Schultz gave up after being turned down by banks 242 times, there would be no Starbucks. If J.K. Rowling stopped after being turned down by multiple publishers for years, there would be no Harry Potter. If Walt Disney quit too soon after his theme park concept was trashed 302 times, there would be no Disneyland.

My life before entrepreneurship was no comparison to the fullness I'm experiencing now once God revealed to me that I'm uniquely called to do this. I used to tremble at the thought of presenting in front of crowds. I used to be so shy with low self-esteem and low confidence. But I persevered through my personal challenges and now I've won several pitch competitions across the country which has brought in vast resources to launch and grow my company. When all else fails, commit to persevere.

R - Restoration

Entrepreneurship and life in general requires daily renewal. It's not a sprint, it's a marathon. Expect to invest the next 5-10 years of your life to seeing your dreams come true. Given the time that it takes, you will surely burn out if you don't renew your mind daily. There was a point in time when I worked no less than 80 hours per week and over time that took a toll on my body and I would run myself into utter exhaustion. Over time your body physically breaks down and when you may be enduring failures and experiencing anxiety or depression on top of that, it's easy to not prioritize restoration and renewal like you should which will leave you stuck and feeling less than yourself. Ways to keep yourself restored along the way is getting enough rest, maintaining a healthy diet, getting adequate exercise, and keeping prayer a daily activity. I let most of these things go as soon as I jumped into entrepreneurship and I suffered greatly because of it. You are going to be pushed outside of your comfort zone as you're manifesting your dreams and different circumstances will try to take you out, but you can be more than a conqueror by staying centered and maintaining a great overall well being. Don't neglect your family and friends along the way because the love these relationships provide is also very nourishing. At the end of the day when you fall short, they will always be there for you and it's important to cherish that. Always make it a priority to stay connected to the ones you love and make self-care an essential daily practice.

I - Intuition

Steve Jobs once said, "Have the courage to follow your heart and intuition. They somehow already know what you truly want to become. Everything else is secondary." The little whispers and nudges from your spirit is designed to supernaturally guide you. Make sure you are not ignoring them because it's not just a coincidence. Your intuition comes to you to help you stay sharp and helps prevent you from making careless mistakes. My intuition has shown up to me in a number of ways like reminding me to double check an address for a meeting, remembering to get that signature documented for a contract, reminding me to send that NDA first before speaking, and the gut feeling I have after the first impression of a person. Your intuition is constantly guiding you, always follow its leading.

I've always contemplated past mistakes where I regret not following my intuition. Sometimes we think it may be too much to work through at the time but trust me, it's best to stop and follow its direction because it's usually trying to prevent you from something that could be even worse. Save yourself from the heartache and do what you have to do.

C - Cash Flow and Character

I use both terms here because not all success is measured monetarily. Success usually has a lot to do with your character. Financial success is nothing without the character to help you sustain it.

Cash flow is an important element of growing a business. It's an indicator of company health that you're creating enough value for people who are paying for your good or service in exchange on a consistent basis. It also indicates how long your company will last based on your monthly expenses and balance sheet. A few years in, we changed our business model because the revenue wasn't at a profit that could sustain the company operations. It was a blessing in disguise because it pushed us to build new technology that will create more value for our customer through personalized hair care recommendations. You can't be afraid to pivot and change your business plan especially when the numbers show that a change is necessary. You're blocking your blessing if you don't learn to pivot when needed.

When you have mastered your model enough and the money is flowing in, it's important to ensure that your character and those around you are filled with integrity and discipline. A few poor decisions could cause you to lose everything you've earned. Without cash flow you don't have a business, but without character you don't have a future.

E - Enthusiasm

You can ask anybody who knows me or who has ever had an encounter with me that I always have a smile on my face. It's because of my passion and that I truly love what I do. When you do something you love, you'll never work a day in your life. I am incredibly enthusiastic about my business, our mission, and vision for our industry and the customers we serve. Having enthusiasm is so important because you have to keep others motivated, you have to excite others in order to draw in resources and persuade others to work with you or help you, and honestly no one likes dull, negative energy. I remember there was a time that I really wanted to work with a huge hair blogger that I absolutely adored and she agreed simply because I captured her interest with my enthusiasm and passion. It's incredibly contagious.

Be enthusiastic about the vision you have for yourself and your business. Just have fun with it! You being called to this is purposeful and bigger than yourself. Envision how the world will be changed by your business or your talents and passions. Envision how people's lives will be transformed and how you can even start a movement for a needed cause. Then, expect it to happen. Expect success and lead with enthusiasm.

Emotional Shift

"He who looks outside dreams, he who looks inside awakens." -- Carl Jung

Facing depression & anxiety

I faced my feelings of depression and anxiety - shifting from emptiness to fullness.

The state of the world is causing an alarming increase in the amount of people experiencing anxiety and depression. Many entrepreneurs and dreamers can also relate to going through the same as the quest to see our visions birthed in reality can be a daunting feat. I share your pain of experiencing the same agony. This scripture really kept me strong as I was dealing with my feelings of depression:

But he said to me, "My grace is sufficient for you, for my power is made perfect in weakness." Therefore I will boast all the more gladly about my weaknesses, so that Christ's power may rest on me.

-- 2 Corinthians 12:9

We all go through circumstances that bring us to our knees in sadness and disappointment and sometimes we stay in that state and it leaves us in a low valley of depression. You are not alone. Sometimes the weight of the world is just too much and we retreat in our own minds without the strength to fight another day. It is in these moments that we can trust and be assured that we can give it over to God. It's also very important to know that it's okay to take a break and rest. Be still. We were purposed to live life abundantly and that applies to our emotions as well. Whenever those depressed feelings start to creep in, I had to check myself and say wait - God has purposed me to live life abundantly and that means in joy and happiness. What am I missing here? Am I trying to do too much? In what ways am I holding on to what I wish could be different? Most of the time depression ensues when we wish that our external circumstances could be different. We may be missing the meaning of the experience that we're going through which is typically a catalyst for change and not a sick punishment.

When depression ensues because of loss, always remember that when grief runs deep, God's comforting love still runs deeper. The peace we long for and the rest we are desperate for will always be found in the arms of Jesus. And those arms are constantly reaching out to us. The Lord is close to the brokenhearted and saves those who are crushed in spirit. A righteous man may have many troubles, but the Lord delivers him from them all. (Psalm 34:18, 19)

My depression came from not seeing things happen in the timeframe that I wanted it to happen. I had to learn that things happen in God's timing, not my deadline. I was refreshed by this passage I found when dealing with the root of my frustration:

God is preparing you. Unfortunately, the path that takes us to the promise is always wrought with thickets and thorns. God allows the path to be difficult because He intends on refining us and preparing us for our place of promise. God loves us too much to promote us before we are ready. On the other side of this refining time is a fresh perspective and new mercies. Humble yourself under the mighty hand of God; in due time you will be lifted up and honored before a watching world.

God's mercies are always available and joy does come in the morning. While I realize it's completely normal for us to process emotions of anxiety and unrest, the Bible says that it is not God's plan for us to crumble in its wake. (2 Timothy 1:7) We can't let fear run our lives, which is one of the main causes of anxiety. Fear was never meant to control or consume us. When dealing with my anxiety, I had to face the fact that it was ultimately coming from a place of fear. A good way to relieve anxiety is by focusing on the present moment and not be fixed on the future. Take a deep breath. Be thankful being alive. Change your vibration by moving to a state of gratitude and think of all the things that you can be grateful for to put things in perspective. This scripture really renewed my mind from anxiety:

"Come to me, all you who are weary and burdened, and I will give you rest. Take my yoke upon you and learn from me, for I am gentle and humble in heart, and you will find rest for your souls." (Matthew 11:28-29)

When you start the day with a refreshed mindset from reading the Bible, you can make anything happen by operating from a higher place of power. It's higher than any depression or anxiety that you experience. If you've contemplated suicide, now is not your time to die. Continue to trust in His unfailing love. We cannot exhaust His supply. His plans are always better for us, to live life abundantly.

Breaking unhealthy attachments

I acknowledged my emotions and dealt with them in a healthy way - the shift from reacting to my emotions with bad habits to developing healthier ways to deal.

I used to have an unhealthy attachment to food. I became an emotional eater and gained a lot of weight. I was embarrassed to even look at some pictures. I was covering up a lot of voids in my life with temporary pleasures and comfort foods. We're living in a society where it's easier to numb the emotions that we feel with everything from food, drugs, and alcohol to prolong our confrontation with the pain. We come to moments in which we're sad, scared, or stressed and it's the best option we have at that time until we develop the strength to face it. I was letting my emotions drive me and I never felt in a state of true peace. I was always running against deadlines, measuring myself against someone else's expectations, wondering how to support myself, and the list went on and on. It was an endless spiral of insanity. I just came to a place where I declared that I didn't want to live like that anymore. I wanted to be free. So I started the journey of asking myself what I was really covering up and being very real with myself. When our emotions start affecting us physically, we have to realize that it is, too, a part of our success to be physically and emotionally strong. God needs us at our best and we must all get to understand ourselves better in our own time to replace bad habits with good ones. I fasted for 40 days doing the Daniel Fast and it completely changed my habits from operating from the flesh to operating from the spirit. The impact of this change manifests in my success on a daily basis.

Past relationships can also serve as unhealthy attachments if you haven't made peace with its' ending whether that be a significant other or a partnership. My favorite book is called A Return To Love by Marianne Williamson and in it she shares such a beautiful perspective on relationships that truly helped me let go of past lovers that didn't work out. In the book she describes how relationships are spiritual encounters with assignments for maximum soul growth at that period of time. Once the purpose of the relationship has been served, separation occurs. I think we get caught up in wanting people to outlast the season they've been purposed to be in our lives. Once they've overstayed their welcome, the friction of staying when you should be separating or evolving creates negative emotions and experiences. You may also be creating a co-dependent relationship with that person if they validate you in a certain way which is a very unhealthy attachment that can stunt your growth or cause you to endure painful things for the sake of "love". You will also be holding space from the right lover to come into your life who could be everything you've ever dreamed of and more. Why stay stuck on one person when God has so much more for you? If someone walks away from you, let them leave. Your destiny isn't tied to anyone who left. The same is true for partnerships. Some people may be meant to work with you for only a certain period of time. Understand how to recognize when someone's season is up. Learn how to not be totally reliant on someone else to do the things you want to do. One should complement but not dominate your existence. Some partnerships are designed to be only for a reason, a season, or in an ongoing fashion. It's important to know when someone's time is up and be confident enough to address it and move on. Always know that "God cuts off every branch that bears no fruit, while every branch that does bear fruit he prunes so that it will be even more fruitful." (John 15:2)

Take responsibility for your life

I took responsibility for my own happiness - the shift from thinking happiness was something I longed for to it being a state I can enjoy right now.

The most genuine thing about myself is my smile. It's my trademark and expression of my spirit. I realized that at one point in time, it was also a mask because I didn't truly feel happy. I was attaching to certain things to keep this illusion of happiness. This gap was created by who I was now and where I felt like I "should" be. Then I realized that no one defines who or what I need to be except for me. I had to take back responsibility for what truly makes me happy and not compare myself to anyone else's standard of happiness. When you're an entrepreneur, you do some pretty unconventional things. You're never in society's box that has been created or even frankly, your family's. You're almost never on any standard timeline when it comes to marriage, kids, financial status, and all the other "adult" milestones that so superficially creates a mirage of happiness, worth, and contentment. I had to take control of how I measure my own happiness, how my own life was unfolding, and just be happy with where I am. I know the uncertainty of life may scare some people when thinking about branching out into the unknown but I see it more as an adventure of the evolution of my purpose and that's what makes me happy. I don't have to wait until that "one day" when it all makes sense and everything works out. I can smile with 100% gratification that I love who I am, what I do, and how I do it. That is success and that is happiness.

The path from who you are to who you envision yourself to be is an incredible journey. Understanding the positive energy that radiates from my own personal happiness helped me develop new trust and agreement with my soul that is described in this affirmation:

By living in my wholeness, I am happy and complete. I commit to protecting the energy that keeps myself happy and whole.

Financial Shift

Know what you want, create a plan on how to get it, and work on it everyday with a burning desire to possess it.
- Think and Grow Rich

The value of money

I learned the true value of money - the shift from a state of it defining who I am to supporting who I want to be.

You can learn to appreciate something when you have to go without it for while. I haven't had a steady paycheck since May 2012. (your response to that sentence alone will show you your true understanding of sacrifice) However, all of my needs have been provided for. God will use times of sacrifice to teach you true value. I couldn't let the absence or presence of money define who I am. I know that God is preparing me for the manifestation of an abundance of wealth that will be distributed and managed in a way that honors Him. It's been repeated over and over in scripture that the only way you can test God is by how you give your money. When He can trust you, He will multiply your finances. When He can trust that you won't squander these blessings that are meant to serve other people, in the drop of a second it will be given.

Coming from the middle class community, it's so important for us to learn how to manage money.

This is an area that is rarely taught to us. Some great books to build your financial intelligence are Think and Grow Rich by Napoleon Hill, The Wealth Choice by Dennis Kimbro, Total Money Makeover by Dave Ramsey, and Real Money Answers by Patrice Washington.

My personal testimony is that I had to release the shackles of financial lack and get comfortable with talking millions, then comfortable with talking billions. I had to quickly realize that sometimes you feel silent to that which you've never experienced. Remind yourself that the universe is abundant and we can change our financial situation when we understand the true value of money and the true value of ourselves - an abundant creation.

Your relationship with money

I changed my relationship with money - shifting from a relationship of dependence to independence.

I have to admit that money used to make me feel insecure. When I felt like I never had enough, it always made me feel less than. I had to learn that money is a tool. It doesn't make us who we are. It's a tool to accomplish things faster (hopefully the right things). It helps us buy time by working with more people (hopefully the right people). It can be here today and gone tomorrow. It can be a mask of your true insecurities. It can be used to put your pride on full display. It can be the root of all evil. It's dangerous to relate to money in a way that defines your sense of self. What tool will it be for you? Many of us have suffered from the poverty mindset. If you're operating in this way, how can you ever attain true wealth? I knew that God had to mold me in a way that changed my relationship with money. One book that was a defining factor in how I learned this was Super Rich by Russell Simmons. Please read it! I was blessed to have a signed copy from him back in 2010. I'm thankful for a friend who had a copy after mines was lost that gave me a sign to read it again. Man, I love how your mind evolves years between readings. He helped me to see again that "everything of quality that you accomplish in your outer, or worldly, life will stem from your inner life." I have a whole new perspective this time around reading it. Here are my top 10 lessons about being Super Rich:

1. Your happiness is going to reside in your gift and your gift alone (not money)
2. Let go of the results. Your only true job is to be awake and focused in the moment. The results of that work belong to God
3. Move through life as a sweet, humble, generous giver
4. You will essentially be skipped to the head of the line through a single display of total faith
5. If money serves us any purpose in this life, it's solely to help alleviate suffering; to feel blissful and free every time I give away a dollar, instead of resentful and tight; to have a simple, happy, uncluttered mind; to live with consciousness and compassion; to be awake and kind; to have a strong "inside- out" game
6. Loving unconditionally is always in your best interest. There should be no limit to our ability to forgive
7. Keep encouraging people to move in the right direction
8. Every new day offers a chance for us to be reborn, a fresh opportunity to move away from our cravings and mistakes and get closer to our higher selves
9. Break free from the sheep mentality

10. Be a builder of bridges that bring people together

Russell helped me to accept that all the ways I had undergone personal development, no matter if it was a pleasure or a pain, was necessary in order to unblock the flow of money into my life and rest in a place of true wealth and abundance.

Income generation

I learned the source of all income generation - the shift from a position of lack to abundance by using my gifts.

Here's how you make money, it's very simple: create value in other people's lives. That's what people pay for. Solve their pain, improve their life, or make their job easier. The beautiful thing is you have already been blessed with gifts and talents that allow you to deliver in one of these ways to a specific group of people. Your only job is to discover what that is. At birth, God gave each person gifts and talents that are of value in this world and meant for the exchange of currency to attract resources. This goes back to the point that our only work is inner work. Once we do the inner work, it manifests in the outer world. There will come a day when you no longer have to even think about money because you're operating in your true purpose and anointing. Let's all get to that place of truly giving ourselves for the positive impact of others. It says in scripture:

"Give, and it will be given to you. A good measure, pressed down, shaken together and running over, will be poured into your lap. For with the measure you use, it will be measured to you." Luke 6:38

Once I understood this, I developed a new affirmation:

I have the ability to produce long-lasting wealth.

My personal testimony of when I began to see a shift with truly knowing the purpose of money and wealth in my life was during an interview with Madame Noire when I was asked the question, "what are you most inspired by?" I answered, "Creating generational wealth for my family and the African-American community as a whole, so that we can overcome poverty and be in a greater position of ownership and economic opportunity." I knew that shift was where I needed to be to properly understand my purpose and responsibility for the wealth that I am preparing myself to receive.

Relational Shift

The people around you can elevate you or destroy you.

Circle of support

I created a tight circle of support - the shift from hanging with everyone to clinging to only those who supported my growth.

The most valuable thing you can have is relationships. Shifting out of your comfort zone can be the most frightening, uncertain thing you can ever experience. It's important to surround yourself with people who will support you during this time of growth. Every person in your life has their own season. Some people won't cling to you during this season and that's okay. Some people will cling to you like never before as your confidant, your pick-me-up when you need it, your help-me-out when you need it, your prayer warrior, and simply put - a good friend. This tribe will be your bridge to shift from one chapter of your life to the next. These will be the people you can trust without a doubt and can call them in the midnight hour when you need it. God has most likely already shown you who you can depend on and who will never second guess this dream you want to bring to fruition. Keep them close.

On the professional side, it's important to identify the right people to line up for optimal company growth. I remember watching this sermon on TV by Bishop Dale Bronner at Word of Faith Church preaching about "The Domino Effect" which symbolizes the right things lined up at the right time in a manner in which God can bless:

1. You must have the dominos (talents, abilities, dreams, visions)
2. You've got to line the dominos up properly (set up your management team, sales strategy, marketing plan, accounting system)
3. Push the first domino over in the right direction
4. When you push over the first domino, get ready for the rest of them to fall in place

The anointing only flows in alignment. Do the right thing at the right time with the right people. Learn how to assemble the right personalities, skills, and tenacity all in alignment with the right mission. When you are obedient and get the right things lined up with the right people, God will move heaven and Earth for you. The opportunity will be given to the man or woman who is ready. The right opportunity opens because the vessel is ready. That is how you should be spending your time, keeping your circle tight as the blueprint is established.

Association

I learned the power of association - shifting from an "I can do it all" mentality and learning to lean on the strength of a team.

When you try to do everything on your own, you rob the blessing from other people to be used by God on this path of dreams to fruition. Other people also need to experience what you're bringing to life and have the skills you need to achieve it. We have to learn the art of delegation. This helped reinforce the importance of relationships and how transparency in communication keeps them strong. Don't be afraid to be wrong and don't be afraid to acknowledge the fact that you need others. The heart of your company is your people and the vibrancy of your life is supported by people.

One entrepreneur that I admire, Lara Hodgson, said this on a panel at a conference I attended that has stuck with me ever since, "Don't hire skill sets, hire mindsets." The right people to associate yourself with on a team can be determined by how they think. It's also important to learn the power of intentional networking as you're out in your field to make the most of the moments that are created by meeting people along your path. I learned this from another entrepreneur, author, and speaker I admire, Patrice Washington, who shared how to be more intentional with the time you spend at events to make the most of building potential relationships:

1. Set intentions before you attend the event by asking yourself the question, what's most important right now to accomplish?
2. Remind yourself of these intentions and don't get distracted
3. Tell people what you need
4. Ask people how you can support them

One of the most powerful things Patrice said was, "There's always someone watching you who has the power to bless you." Learn the power of associating with the right people and building the right team to open fruitful relationships in your life.

Always remember to follow up with every person that you meet. It leaves an imprint in their minds that can be recalled when an opportunity is searching for your name. The power of relationships is what led to our first national TV appearance on the Melissa Harris- Perry show. Sometimes it's not about who you know but who knows you. That's why it's of utmost importance to make a favorable impression in every encounter.

Disassociation

I learned the necessity of disassociation - the shift from being a people pleaser to knowing when someone's time is up.

I truly love when Paul says in the bible:

"Obviously, I'm not trying to win the approval of people, but of God. If pleasing people were my goal, I would not be Christ's servant."
— Galatians 1:10 NLT

So many of us keep people in our lives when their reason or season is up. We avoid having uncomfortable conversations and we justify people's actions. The only thing this does is block our blessings when God is calling you to do more and be more. I used to be the queen of people pleasing. It comes from my childhood of being such a good student and good child that developed a condition of wanting the approval of others because I had naturally cultivated that attitude from others by just simply having a spirit of excellence. As you grow, you must understand how to change certain behaviors that have outgrown their season in order to move into a new level of relationship building. The things that serve you as a child no longer serve you as an adult. This is a maturity stage that some of us never fully grow out of.

You can understand when someone's season is up by how they treat you and how you receive their behavior towards you. Does it make you feel empowered? Do they honor your time? Do you feel a constant sense of frustration? Sometimes your standards are no longer met and by not dismissing them from your space, your energy only breeds a constant state of discontentment. It's important to address these issues heads on - in your personal life and professional life.

When people show you who they are, believe them the first time. We can thank the great Maya Angelou for this moment of telling it like it is. We can also be grateful when people show their true colors! It's okay when people ruffle your feathers, it's a way to get your attention. We so often think it has something to do with us when it's just God's way of giving you a sign that they no longer serve your higher purpose. It is what it is. These are the ebbs and flows of life, relationships come and they go. That's why we can be grateful for those who show us they mean no good for us.

Come to a place of clarity in knowing who is truly for you. You may have to take a step back for a while from your normal environment to have this moment of clarity. Retain your respect for the person. We all have ways that we need to grow. But it's important to let that person go because it's blocking your blessings.

Once I gained the strength of letting people go, I developed a new affirmation:

I will accept the natural flow of friends, associates, and foes in and out of my circle.

Spiritual Shift

"We were born to make manifest the glory of God that is within us. It's not just in some of us; it's in everyone. And as we let our own light shine, we unconsciously give other people permission to do the same. As we are liberated from our own fear, our presence automatically liberates others."
-- Marianne Williamson

Overcoming fear

I recognized that my fears don't really exist - the shift from living in fear to living with a fearless mentality.

In every moment that we make a choice or take an action, we are operating from a place of standing in fear or standing in love. One of the most profound things I've learned from my favorite author and spiritual leader Marianne Williamson is a mind shift that states, "I am willing to see this differently." Every time I face a fear I tell myself I am willing to see this differently.

Let's talk about the fear of failure. It mostly stems from resistance to failure and if we can just accept it as part of the process, that resistance will ultimately disappear. All failure is not fatal. Failures are meant to be learning lessons and stepping stones.
Whenever I feel nervous, I realize that I'm letting fear breed in me. We must nip it in the bud so that we don't hold ourselves back and sabotage our own success. Fear is false evidence appearing real so

please take a moment to say goodbye to your fears as you read on.

Prayer is a great replacement for worrying which is a symptom of fear. Prayer will change your situation and it will change you. Active prayer demonstrates that you know God is in control. Once you do that, He in turn gives you his peace to operate in the midst of what used to be your fear. This shift personifies what is declared in scripture that says, "I can do all things through Christ who strengthens me." (Phil 4:13) He gives you the strength to move in action in a manner that liberates you from your fears and answers your prayer. It is at this point that you can truly do all the things you've ever imagined.

Finding faith

I took steps of faith over and over again - the shift to a lifestyle of walking by faith and letting God lead the way.

God continuously pointed out areas in which I need to operate in faith just a little more. Given the fact that I'm a first time entrepreneur, everything that I've done required stepping out into the unknown and coming to a place of truly trusting God in order to endure the journey. My actions weren't showing the faith in which I believed I had. Why do you try to do everything in your own strength if you truly trust God to provide? You can't outwork God's grace. My time of rest was a time to prove to God that I will continue to trust Him. One act of obedience to God can completely change the trajectory of your life. You have no idea the plans God has for you once you demonstrate that He can trust you.

How can you demonstrate faith? Keep giving even though you're not receiving. Honor God even though things are not changing. Keep getting stronger under pressure, knowing faith grows under the fire of affliction.

God prepares you for new levels during time periods of building your faith. Character is developed under tough times. Until He removes you from your situation, stay in faith. When you stay faithful in the wilderness, God can trust you to be faithful in the promised land. Keep having that spirit of excellence. Stay happy and joyful even when God doesn't take your circumstances away. If God is not removing the frustration, there is a reason. His grace and mercy will continue to keep you.

Hebrews 11 provides great examples of faith in action. In verses 1-3, it tells us that:

"Faith is confidence in what we hope for and assurance about what we do not see. This is what the ancients were commended for. By faith we understand that the universe was formed at God's command, so that what is seen was not made out of what was visible."

And so it is with the manifestation of our dreams. For time periods that can draw on for years, we cannot see it. But faith sees the invisible, feels the intangible, and achieves the impossible.

Seeing purpose in your pain

I was willing to open to my areas of pain to replace with God's purpose - the shift from endless pain to transformed purpose.

I traded in my sorrow for joy and ashes for beauty. I had an out-of-body experience that saw myself completely healed and completely whole and observed that she was who the world needed to accomplish God's mission for her life. There is purpose in your pain. That's the beauty of life. When you pursue your purpose, you're honoring the reason God placed you on this Earth. Why wouldn't He bless that tremendously? There is glory from your story. I remember the exact day I was healed from all of my past hurts. I was reading my daily devotional like normal but this time the words connected with my soul and spirit on a level that I knew was designed especially for me. It was from the scripture Mark 5:34:

He said to her, "Daughter, your faith has healed you. Go in peace and be freed from your suffering."

I knew God was releasing me from all that was continuing to hold me captive from all that I was called to be. We must be freed from our past to take hold of the newness of life that is granted to us from the birth of our dreams in the physical realm. There's no need to suffer from your past mistakes and hurts. Be free and receive God's promises.

I developed a new affirmation:

I will trust God's divine purpose and plan for my life no matter how hard life gets. I'm thankful for this journey for it is how God has prepared me for my destiny.

There are many steps you have to take before you are ready for your blessing. If we get what God has in store for us too soon, we can't handle it. He who has begun a good work in you will complete it until the day of Jesus Christ. (Philippians 1:6)

Outro

So let's begin the shift

I have a dream of seeing all those around me live life more abundantly. These 5 ½ years have been an important foundation and time of sowing in order to reap a harvest. This scripture spoke directly to coming out of this time of reflection:

"Watch out! Remember the three years I was with you—my constant watch and care over you night and day, and my many tears for you. And now I entrust you to God and the message of his grace that is able to build you up and give you an inheritance with all those he has set apart for himself."

Acts of the Apostles 20:31-32 NLT

You don't have to start your quest today, but you can get started with planning. I thank God for saving me for my purpose and that I was kept through all the trials and tribulations along the way. These are the steps I've taken to grow and make a shift personally, professionally, mentally, financially, relationally, emotionally, and spiritually throughout my journey. We must continue living life courageously and keep on claiming the victory. Accept the facts when you fail and learn from it. It's a seed for the next stage of growth.

Don't waste another day just doing the next thing. Take a long, hard look at your work, your job, and your agenda to make sure you are in the right place doing what you were created to do in this world, for it says in the Bible:

"I know the plans I have for you," declares the LORD, "plans to prosper you and not to harm you, plans to give you hope and a future." (Jer 29:11 NIV)

Consider how you will make a shift in your life by taking the following steps:

- Take time to discover your purpose
- Seek God and ask for His direction
- Seek His will by searching His Word
- Pay attention to the passions of your heart
- Realistically evaluate your abilities and skills
- Take into account your natural talents
- Consider the advice of those who know you best

- Step out in faith, trusting God to help you make the right choice

God is preparing you. Humble yourself and seek to understand what the Lord is doing around you. Take as long as it takes, not according to the time in which you "think" something should be happening. The universe will lay the path right out for you. God will faithfully lead you and you will be strengthened as you go. And ultimately, let us commit.

"So let's not get tired of doing what is good. At just the right time we will reap a harvest of blessing if we don't give up." Galatians 6:9 NLT

The Shift Plan

Fill in the blank:

It's my time to: _____
_____.

Make the shift in every area of your life.

Personal Shift

Self-Assessment: I made a personal commitment to better myself - the shift from avoiding my flaws to embracing them for true change.

Introspective Inventory: I took an introspective inventory of my strengths and weaknesses - the shift from passive awareness to intentional application.

Affirmation & Belief: I created affirmations and renewed belief in myself - the shift from lingering defeating thoughts to active empowering thoughts.

Professional Shift

Career Change: I prayerfully prepared for my career change - the shift from a full-time employee to a startup entrepreneur.

Real Leadership: I committed to work on my leadership skills - shifting from company associate to CEO.

Work Ethic: I leveled up on my work ethic without complaints or excuses - the shift from clocking out to doing whatever it takes to get the job done.

Mental Shift

Let Go Of The Slavery Mentality: I recognized old cycles of slavery mentality and uprooted the habits that held me back from my breakthrough - the shift from suffering to breaking free.

Heal From Your Childhood Wounds: I dealt with pains I experienced as a child that were influencing my behavior in adulthood - the shift from being controlled by the past to healing my present and future.

Understand The Real Price of Success: I created my own definition of success - the shift from what society defines as successful to understanding what success really is.

Emotional Shift

Facing Depression & Anxiety: I faced my feelings of depression and anxiety - shifting from emptiness to fullness.

Breaking Unhealthy Attachments: I acknowledged my emotions and dealt with them in a healthy way - the shift from reacting to my emotions with bad habits to developing healthier ways to deal.

Take Responsibility For Your Life: I took responsibility for my own happiness - the shift from thinking happiness was something I longed for to it being a state I can enjoy right now.

Financial Shift

The Value of Money: I learned the true value of money - the shift from a state of it defining who I am to supporting who I want to be.

Your Relationship With Money: I changed my relationship with money - shifting from a relationship of dependence to independence.

Income Generation: I learned the source of all income generation - the shift from a position of lack to abundance by using my gifts.

Relational Shift

Circle of Support: I created a tight circle of support - the shift from hanging with everyone to clinging to only those who supported my growth.

Association: I learned the power of association - shifting from an "I can do it all" mentality and learning to lean on the strength of a team.

Disassociation: I learned the necessity of disassociation - the shift from being a people pleaser to knowing when someone's time is up.

Spiritual Shift

Overcoming Fear: I recognized that my fears don't really exist - the shift from living in fear to living with a fearless mentality.

Finding Faith: I took steps of faith over and over again - the shift to a lifestyle of walking by faith and letting God lead the way.

Seeing Purpose In Your Pain: I was willing to open to my areas of pain to replace with God's purpose - the shift from endless pain to transformed purpose.

Made in the USA
San Bernardino, CA
23 June 2020